CHRIS BRADY

THE BABY BIBLE FOR BEGINNERS IN
MICROSOFT EXCEL

Excel
2013

Discover and share insights
from your data.

A quick thank you……..

Before I begin, I would like to thank you very much for purchasing this eBook. It's taken much trial and error to produce something that will truly benefit anyone starting out using Microsoft excel. I wish I had a book like this available to me when I first started.

Enjoy reading and good luck in your excel career.

Table of Contents

Introduction 4

Formatting Cells 8

Writing Formulas and Expressions 10

Interpreting Cell References in Formulas and Functions 13

Linking Speadsheet Data 15

Cool Keyboard Shortcuts 20

Using Auto Fill Features 22

Creating A Chart 28

Chart Types 31

Customizing Charts 37

Discount Excel Online Course 43

Introduction

An Excel worksheet, or spreadsheet, is a two-dimensional grid with columns and rows. Look at the spreadsheet below. The column names are letters of the alphabet starting with A, and the rows are numbered chronologically starting with the number one. The cells in the first *row* are A1, B1, C1, and so on. And the cells in the first *column* are A1, A2, A3, and so on. These are called cell names or cell references. We use **cell references** when creating math formulas or functions. For example, the formula to add the contents of cells B2 and B3 together is: **=B2+B3**.

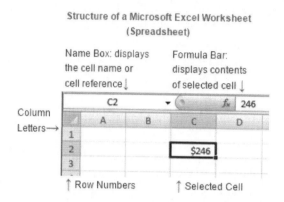

Structure of a Microsoft Excel Worksheet (Spreadsheet)

The **Name Box** is located in the area above Column A, and displays the selected cell - the cell you've clicked in and where the cursor is resting. In our spreadsheet above, the selected cell is C2. Notice that the column letter (C) and the row number (2) change color. The beginning of the **Formula Bar** can be seen in the area above Column D on our worksheet. The Formula Bar displays the contents of the selected cell. A workbook is a collection of worksheets or spreadsheets. When the Excel program is opened, a workbook opens with three blank worksheets. The names of the worksheets are displayed on tabs at the bottom of the Excel window.

Moving From Cell to Cell

The arrow keys can be used to move left, right, up, and down from the current cell. Press the Enter key to move to the cell immediately below the current cell, and press the Tab key to move one cell to the right.

Selecting Cells

There are a variety of ways to select cells in an Excel spreadsheet:

- To select one cell, click in the cell.
- To select one or more rows of cells, click on the row number(s).
- To select one or more columns of cells, click on the column letter(s).

- To select a group of contiguous cells, click in a corner cell and, with the left mouse button depressed, drag the cursor horizontally and/or vertically until all of the cells you want selected are outlined in black.
- To select multiple cells that are not contiguous, press and hold the Ctrl key while clicking in the desired cells.
- To select every cell in the worksheet, click in the upper right corner of the worksheet to the left of "A."

Entering Data into Cells

To enter data into a cell, just click in the cell and begin typing. What you type also displays in the Formula Bar. When entering dates, Excel defaults to the current year if the year portion of the date is not entered. You may edit cell contents from the Formula bar, or from directly inside the cell. To edit from the Formula Bar, select the cell and click inside the Formula Bar. When done typing, either press the Enter key or click inside another cell. To edit directly inside a cell, either double click inside the cell, or select the cell and press the F2 key. Each cell has a specific format. This format tells Excel how the data inside the cell should be displayed.

Propagating Cell Contents

There are multiple ways to propagate or fill data from one cell to adjacent cells. Let's begin with two popular keyboard shortcuts that allow us to *fill down*, or *fill to the right*:

- To fill adjacent cells with the *contents of the cell above*, select the cell with the data and the cells to be filled and press Ctrl + D (the Ctrl key and the D key) to *fill down*.
- To fill adjacent cells with the *contents of the cell to the left*, select the cell with the data and cells to be filled and press Ctrl + R (the Ctrl key and the R key) to *fill to the right*.

To propagate in any direction, use the **Fill Handle**. Click in a cell with data to be copied, hover the cursor over the cell's lower right corner until the cursor changes to a thin plus sign (+) or a dark square, and drag up, down, left, or right to fill the cells. If the data to be copied is a *date, number, time period, or a custom-made series*, the data will be **incremented by one** instead of just copied when the Fill Handle is used. For example, to display the months of the year in column A, type January in cell A1, drag the Fill Handle down to cell A12, and the months will display, in order, in column A!

Moving and Copying Cells

To move cell contents, right-click in the selected cell and click Cut. To copy cell contents, click Copy. Then right-click in the new location and click Paste. To paste a group of cells, right-click in the cell where the *top left cell* of the group should be located, and click Paste. Remove the animated border around the original cell by pressing the ESC key, or start typing in a new cell.

Adding and Deleting Rows and Columns

To insert a new row in a spreadsheet, right-click on a row number, and click Insert. Excel always inserts the row ABOVE the row that was clicked on. To delete a row, right-click on the row number, and click Delete.

To insert a new column, right-click on a column letter and click Insert. Excel always inserts the column to the LEFT of the column that was clicked on. To delete a column, right-click on the column letter, and click Delete.

Protecting a Worksheet (Spreadsheet) or Workbook

To protect a worksheet or workbook in Excel 2007, click the Review tab, click Protect Worksheet or Protect Workbook, and click OK (entering a password first, if desired). When a worksheet or workbook is already protected, the icons in the Review tab are Unprotect Worksheet and Unprotect Workbook. In earlier versions of Excel, click Tools > Protection, click Protect Sheet or Protect Workbook, and click OK (entering a password first, if desired). When a worksheet or workbook is already protected, the menu items read Unprotect Sheet and Unprotect Workbook. Don't enter a password unless absolutely necessary. If you forget the password, you won't be able to unprotect the worksheet, so you won't be able to change, delete, or format any of the Locked cells!

Working with Worksheets (Spreadsheets)

Viewing, Renaming, Inserting, and Deleting Worksheets:
Worksheet tabs are found in the bottom left area of the workbook. **To view a worksheet**, click on its tab. If the workbook window is not wide enough to display all of the tabs, use the arrows to the left of the tabs to navigate left or right, or right-click on any of the arrows and select the tab from the list that displays.
To rename a spreadsheet, right-click on the spreadsheet tab, select Rename from the context menu, and type a new name. Or, double-click on the worksheet tab and type a new name.
To insert a worksheet, right-click on a worksheet tab and select Insert from the menu. Excel always inserts the spreadsheet *to the left of the current worksheet*.
To delete a worksheet, right-click on the worksheet tab and select Delete from the context menu.

Moving Worksheets (Spreadsheets)
Sometimes we want our spreadsheets to be arranged in a different order. **To move a worksheet in the same workbook**, right-click on the tab of the source worksheet and click "Move or Copy." In the Move or Copy window, click the name of the worksheet that you want the sheet to be *inserted before*, and click OK.
To move a spreadsheet to a new workbook, right-click on the tab of the source spreadsheet and click "Move or Copy." In the Move or Copy window, click the drop-down arrow under "To Book:" and click (new book). Excel removes the worksheet from the existing workbook and opens a new workbook containing the moved worksheet.
To move a worksheet to another existing workbook, we recommend copying the worksheet as instructed below, and then deleting the original sheet when the worksheet has been successfully pasted. Using cut and paste is an option, but if something happens to the PC before pasting occurs, a valuable worksheet could be lost.

Copying Worksheets (Spreadsheets)
Rather than start from scratch, it is often easier to copy, and then modify, an existing worksheet. To copy a worksheet in the same workbook, right-click on the tab of the source worksheet and click "Move or Copy." In the Move or Copy window, check the "create a copy" box, click the name of the spreadsheet that you want the sheet to be inserted before, and click OK.

To copy a worksheet into a new workbook, right-click on the tab of the source worksheet and click "Move or Copy." In the Move or Copy window, click the drop-down arrow under "To Book:" and click (new book). Excel opens a new workbook containing the copied spreadsheet.

To copy a worksheet from one workbook to another existing workbook, right-click the top left corner cell to select all cells and click Copy. Open the other Excel workbook, find an empty worksheet, right-click the top left corner cell to select all cells, and click Paste. Return to the first worksheet and press ESC to remove the animated border.

In Closing...

Excel error messages begin with a pound sign (#). The most common error, #####, indicates that the cell is too narrow to display all of the data. Make the column wider by placing the cursor on the right side of the column heading and dragging the column edge to the right.

Formatting Cells

Each cell in a worksheet can be formatted with many properties. As mentioned above, changing the format of a cell doesn't affect the cell value that Excel uses when performing calculations. For example, you may have a cell formatted to display a number with no decimal points. But if cell content is a mathematical formula containing division, the actual cell value may contain many decimal points. There are six tabs in the "Format Cells" window, and all formatting options may be found on one of these tabs. Multiple cells can be formatted in one step by first selecting the cells. The "Format Cells" window can be accessed in all versions of Excel from the right-click menu. In Excel 2007 and 2010, some formatting options are available on the Home Tab on the Font, Alignment, and Number groups. To see formatting options not displayed, click the little arrow in the lower right corner of the group and the "Format Cells" window displays.

How to Format Cells

Number:
The first tab is Number and contains categories for the type of data that is in the cell. The default category is General, and other popular categories are Number, Currency, Date, Percentage, and Text. Some categories have additional options, such as the number of decimal places, how to display negative numbers, and which currency symbol to display, if any. The categories Fraction, Scientific, Accounting, Special, and Custom are also available. The default category, General, is very flexible. Dates display as dates, text displays as text, and numbers display as numbers. Don't indiscriminately format large portions of a spreadsheet with a different category or you may end up reformatting cells and re-entering data. For example, if a date is entered into a cell formatted for currency, the date's serial number will display. If a formula is entered into a cell formatted for a date, the answer will not display. The cell will have to be reformatted and the formula re-entered.

Alignment:
The second tab is Alignment. Use the options on this tab to align text in the cell, indent text, wrap text, and merge cells. Text direction and text orientation in degrees can also be specified.

Font:
The third tab is Font and the usual options are presented. Font, font style, color, size, underline style, and special effects.

Border:
The fourth tab is Border. The Border tab provides a variety of border styles, and any color may be selected for a border. A border style and border color can be set for each side of an individual cell or a group of cells. Many folks have trouble applying a border style or color because Excel is fussy about the order in which steps are taken. Always select the border style and color first; then select the side or sides of the cell to receive the border by clicking one of the presets or clicking one or more sides of the box. A cell or group of cells can have four borders - each with a different color and style.

Patterns or Fill:

The fifth tab is called Patterns or Fill - depending on the version of Excel. The background of cells can be filled with any imaginable color, a colored pattern, or a custom gradient. These options can make a worksheet more attractive, and techniques like shading every other row with a light gray color or simple pattern can make spreadsheet data easier to read.

Protection:

The last tab is Protection. This feature allows the user to define certain cells as Locked and/or Hidden. A Locked cell cannot be formatted, nor can its contents be changed or deleted. This is a great feature for preventing formulas and functions from being accidently changed or erased. When a Hidden cell is selected, its contents do not display in the Formula Bar, but they can still be deleted. All cells are locked by default. To unlock all but a few cells, click in the top-left cell of the worksheet to select all cells, right-click and select "Format Cells," and remove the checkmark in the Lock box. Then lock individual cells that need protection.

IMPORTANT: In order for the Lock or Hidden option to go into effect, the **worksheet or workbook must be Protected.**

Writing Formulas and Expressions

Whenever the contents of the cells referenced in a math formula change, Excel will automatically recalculate the answer for you. That is what makes this software program so powerful. As some formulas can get extremely complicated, it is a good idea to lock those cells that contain the formulas and protect the worksheet. A cell, or a group of cells, can be locked via the Protection tab on the Format window.

The 5 basic rules to remember as we discuss Excel formulas are:

1. All Excel formulas start with an equal (=) sign. This tells Excel that it is a formula.
2. The answer to the formula displays in the cell into which the formula is entered.
3. Cells are referenced in a formula by their column-row identifier, ie. A1, B2.
4. The symbols for addition, subtraction, multiplication, and division are: + - * /
5. You do not have to enter capital letters in your formula; Excel will automatically capitalize them.

Example of simple math formulas:

- =A1+A6   this Excel formula adds the contents of cell A1 and A6
- =A1+A2+A3   this Excel formula adds the contents of the three cells specified. (See the SUM function for adding multiple numbers)
- =A3-A1   this Excel formula subtracts the contents of cell A1 from the contents of cell A3
- =B2*B3   this Excel formula multiples the numbers in cells B2 and B3
- =G5/A5   this Excel formula divides G5 by A5. (NOTE: If you see the error message #DIV/O! in a cell, you are trying to divide by zero or a null value - which is not allowed.)
- =G5^2   this formula tells Excel to square the value in cell G5. The number *after* the caret is the exponent. Likewise, the formula H2^3 would cube the value in cell H2.

We can combine multiple operations in one formula. Make sure you use parentheses where needed or you may not get the correct results (see Order of Operations below). Here are some examples:

- =(C1+C3)/C4   This Excel formula adds the value in C1 to the value in C3, and then divides the result by the value in C4
- =4*(A2+A5)+3   This Excel formula adds the contents of A2 and A5, multiples this sum by 4, and then adds 3.

Mathematical Order of Operations

Remember the Order of Operations by remembering the phrase **P**lease **E**xcuse **M**y **D**ear **A**unt **S**ally. The letters stand for: Parentheses, Exponents, Multiplication, Division, Addition, and Subtraction. And all operations are carried out from **left** to **right**. Here is how the order is applied:

1. First, any math inside of parentheses is calculated.
2. On the second pass, all exponents are resolved.
3. Then any multiplication OR division is performed.
4. Lastly, any addition OR subtraction is performed.

Note: Even though the Aunt Sally phrase may imply that multiplication is done before division, and addition is done before subtraction, that is not true. They are performed during the same step, or pass, through the formula.

Let's illustrate with a simple formula: 4+2*3

- Pass 1 - Since the multiplication must be done first, our expression resolves itself to 4+6=10.

Let's practice with a more complex formula: (2*4)+3^2-8/4

- Pass 1 - Parentheses: 2*4 = 8. Now our expression reads: 8+3^2-8/4
- Pass 2 - Exponents: 3^2=9. Now our expression reads: 8+9-8/4
- Pass 3 - Multiply and Divide: 8/4=2. Now our expression reads: 8+9-2
- Pass 4 - Add and Subtract: The answer is 15

Now test your skill on a complicated formula! 3^(6/3)+(3*3)-2*(6-3)

- Pass 1 - Parentheses: 6/3=2, 3*3=9, and 6-3=2. So now our formula reads: 3^2+9-2*3
- Pass 2 - Exponents: 3^2=9. So now our formula reads: 9+9-2*3
- Pass 3 - Multiply and Divide: 2*3=6. So now our formula reads: 9+9-6
- Pass 4 - Add and Subtract: 12

Calculating Percentages in Excel

There are two ways to calculate percentages in Excel, depending on how the worksheet (spreadsheet) is designed.

Display a Percent Sign in the Cell
To calculate a percentage and have the percent sign display in the cell, just enter the formula in the cell and *format the cell as a Percentage*. Let's suppose the formula in cell C2 is =A2/B2. If A2=25 and B2=50, then 25÷50=.5 and .5 will display in cell C2. However, format C2 as a Percentage and 50% will display instead. As we learned in our beginner's tutorial, Excel Made Easy, to format a cell or group of cells, right-click in the cell and click "Format Cells...." Click "Percentage" on the Number tab, indicate the number of decimal points, if any, and click "OK."

Use a Column Heading of Percent and No Percent Sign in the Cell
Let's suppose you're dividing the values in column A by the values in column B, putting the answers in column C, and column C has a column heading of PERCENT. Using the example above, we would want "50" to display in cell C2, not .5. To express percentages in a cell, multiply by 100. In our example, our

new formula would be =(A2/B2)*100. Excel will divide A2 by B2 and get .5, then multiple .5 by 100 and display the answer, 50, in cell C2.

Copying and Pasting Formulas

To copy the contents of a cell, click in the cell, right-click, and click Copy. (Or use the keyboard shortcut Ctrl+C.) Then place the cursor in the receiving cell, right-click, and click Paste. (Or use the keyboard shortcut Ctrl+V.) To remove the animated border on the original cell, press Enter, press the Esc key, or click in another cell and begin typing. When pasting the contents of a cell into multiple cells, the cell contents need only be copied once. Use the arrows on the keyboard to move to the other cells and paste.

Final Thoughts

When performing calculations, the resulting number may, at times, be quite large - as when dividing numbers. If the number is too large to fully display in the cell, you may see ##### in the cell. When this happens, either make the cell wider, change the cells display font, or format the cell to display fewer decimal points.

Interpreting Cell References in Formulas and Functions

Excel interprets cell references in formulas in a 'relational' manner. It looks at how cells *relate to each other, positionally, on the grid.* This is good news! Let's see why. Let's calculate some simple column totals. We will add the contents of A1 to A2, and put the answer in A3. So in cell A3 we will type the formula =A1+A2. See the image below.

A3			f_x	=A1+A2	
	A	B	C	D	E
1	10	16	22	12	9
2	5	4	2	4	3
3	15				

This is how Excel interprets the formula in cell A3: **"Take the number in the cell *two cells above my current position,* add it to the number in the cell *one cell above my current position,* and put the answer *in this cell."* This is very handy when copying and pasting formulas into worksheet cells as you will see below. Also, notice in the image above how a cell's contents, including the formula, is always displayed in the white box or **formula bar** at the top of the Excel spreadsheet.

The Effect on Cell References When Copying Formulas

As we just learned, Excel interprets cell references relationally. Because of this, when a formula is copied from one cell to another, Excel will *change the cell names in order to keep the same relationships!* For example, if we copy the formula in cell A3 (=A1+A2) and paste it into cell B3, Excel will change the formula to read **=B1+B2**. And if the formula is pasted into cell F3, Excel will change the formula to **=F1+F2**. Can you see how useful this aspect is when we so often want to total or sub-total the data values in a series of rows or columns? When pasting the contents of a cell into multiple cells, just click on the cell containing the formula, copy it, and paste into the remaining cells - using the arrow keys on the keyboard to move from cell to cell.

How to Use an Absolute Cell Reference in Excel

What if you want to copy a formula but DON'T want Excel to automatically change one or more of the cell references? In these instances you will want to use an **absolute cell reference** in your formula. In the sample spreadsheet below, we want to divide each number in Row 2 by the number in A1, and place the answers in Row 3. Normally, the formula in cell A3 would be =A2/A1. However, if you copy and paste this formula into B3, Excel will change the formula to =B2/B1 and we don't want this! We need the formula in cell B2 to read =B2/A1.

B3			f_x	=B2/$A$1	
	A	B	C	D	E
1	4				
2	24	16	48	8	44
3	6	4			

We tell Excel NOT to change A1 in the formula by using an *absolute cell reference* for A1. To specify an absolute cell reference, place a $ before the column letter and row number of the cell. The formula in cell A3 should now read =A2/$A$1. When copying and pasting the formula into other cells, Excel will keep A1 constant. Notice in our sample worksheet above that the formula in cell B3 shown in the formula bar is =B2/$A$1.

Linking Speadsheet Data

In Excel, a link is a formula that dynamically pulls in data from a cell in another worksheet. The worksheet can be in the same workbook or a different workbook. The **destination worksheet** contains the link formula, and it receives data from a cell in the **source worksheet**. Any time the cell value in the source worksheet changes, the cell containing the link formula will be updated as well the next time it is opened. This is just one of many reasons the Excel software program is so powerful.

Why Link Spreadsheet Data?

The ability to create links often eliminates the need to have identical data entered and updated in multiple sheets. This saves time, reduces errors, and improves data integrity. For example, a company's prices can be stored in a 'Master Price List' worksheet, and others needing pricing data can link to that worksheet. Consider a Sales Manager who has a detailed spreadsheet for each salesperson, but would like a summary sheet to compare salespersons' performance and create grand totals. The summary sheet (destination) would bring in data from all the salespersons' sheets (source).

How to Create the Worksheet Link

Tip: Before creating the link, format the cell containing the link formula in the destination worksheet to equal the format of the source data.

METHOD ONE

1. In the source worksheet, select the cell you want to link to and click the Copy button on the Home tab. Or press Ctrl+C, or right-click and select Copy.
2. Switch to the destination spreadsheet and click the cell where you want the link. Then, depending on your version of Excel:
   - Excel 2007, 2010, and 2013: On the Home tab, click the down arrow below Paste and click Paste Link. In newer versions you may also right-click and select the Paste Link from the Paste menu.
   - Excel 2003 and older versions: On the Edit menu, click Paste Special, and then click Paste Link.
3. Return to the source worksheet and press ESC to remove the animated border around the cell.

METHOD TWO

This is a fast method that works in a different order than Method One.

1. In the destination worksheet cell that will contain the link formula, enter an equal sign (=).
2. In the source worksheet, click in the cell that contains the data and press the Enter key.

Linking a Range of Cells

To link a range of cells in the spreadsheet, select the cells and click the Copy button. In the destination worksheet, click the cell where you want the upper-left cell of the range of cells to be located. Then Paste Link as directed above.

Link Formula Example

In the example below, using Method One, we click in cell B6 in the source worksheet and click Copy. Then, on the destination worksheet, we click in cell B3, and paste the link. The value ($3,500) automatically displays. We follow the same steps to link the data from the Denver and Seattle worksheets to the Store Totals worksheet. And we first formatted the cells to display the data as Currency.

Source Worksheet

	A	B	C
1	Atlanta Store	Date-->	08/20/09
2		$ Collected	
3	Register #1	$1,300	
4	Register #2	$1,000	
5	Register #3	$1,200	
6	Total:	$3,500	------------ Copy

Atlanta / Denver / Seattle / Totals

Destination Worksheet

	A	B	C
1	Store Totals for:		08/20/09
2		$ Collected	
3	Atlanta	$3,500	------Paste as a Link
4	Denver	$2,900	
5	Seattle	$3,200	
6	Total:	$9,600	

Atlanta / Denver / Seattle / Totals

Manually Entering Link Formulas into Spreadsheets

When linking cells in worksheets that are in the same workbook, you can easily enter the formula manually. The link formula, after the equal sign (=), contains the sheet name followed by an exclamation mark (!), and then the cell reference or address:=SheetName!CellReference. The formula in our example is =Atlanta!B6. If the worksheets are in different workbooks in the same folder (directory), the formula also contains the workbook name in brackets. The formula is: =[Filename.xlsx]Sheetname!CellReference. If you use the default file extension in Excel 2007, 2010, and 2013, the extension will be xlsx. Older version use a file extension of xls. If the workbooks are in different folders, the formula would have to include the complete file path as well, so it is best to avoid manual formulas in this situation.

Recommendations When Creating Worksheet Links

Worksheet Locations
Before creating your links, consider where your Excel files are stored. If all of the worksheets are in the same workbook, moving the workbook to a different folder or even a different computer should not be a problem. But if you move either the source or destination workbook to a different folder, the link will break! Also, companies that store worksheets on network servers have additional factors to consider.

Protect the Link Formulas in Your Spreadsheets
When you have formulas in spreadsheets, it is important to protect them from accidental deletion. All cells are locked by default, but the feature has no effect until you *Protect the Worksheet*.

Notate Link Locations in Worksheets
There is no method in Excel to see which cells contain links, so notate in some manner the link locations. One method is to format the cells containing links with a particular fill color. Another way is to document somewhere on the spreadsheet which cells contain links.

Ensure Automatic Calculation is Turned On
Most Excel users want the link formula to automatically update when the source is updated. To ensure that this will happen, follow the following steps depending on your version of Excel:
In Excel 2007, 2010, and 2013:

1. Click the Excel button in the upper left corner.
2. Click the Excel Options button at the bottom of the window.
3. Click Formulas on the left sidebar menu.
4. In the "Calculation Options" section, make sure "Automatically" is checked.

In versions prior to Excel 2007:

1. From the top menu line, click Tools.
2. Click Options.
3. Click the Calculation tab and click Automatic under Calculation.

Avoid Circular Links
A circular link is a condition where a link on Worksheet A references source data on Worksheet B, and a link on Worksheet B references source data on Worksheet A. This is not prohibited, but can make both worksheets very slow to open and update, so Microsoft recommends against it.

Microsoft Office Security Warning

When you open the destination spreadsheet, you may get a security warning that "Automatic update of links has been disabled" as shown in the image below. This often happens in the newer versions of Microsoft Excel.

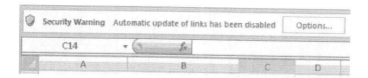

To bypass this warning, press the Options button in the upper right corner. Microsoft will display a Security Alert similar to the image below, warning that if you enable automatic update of links, your computer may no longer be secure. Assuming there actually is no risk ... and to allow the linking process to proceed, click the radio button by "Enable this content" and click OK.

Disable Security Alerts When Linking Worksheets

If you do not want to go through this process each time you open a destination worksheet, disable the alert by following these steps:

- Click "Open the Trust Center" in the lower left corner of the window displayed above and click the External Content tab
- In the second section, click "Enable automatic update for all Workbook Links"

Cool Keyboard Shortcuts

Some shortcut descriptions refer to a "selected" cell. To select a cell, click in the cell. To select multiple cells, press and hold the left mouse button in a corner cell, drag the cursor horizontally and/or vertically to the end of the area, and release the mouse button.

Moving Between Cells

Enter ⇒ Finalize a cell entry and *move to the cell below.*.
Shift + Enter ⇒ Finalize a cell entry and *move to the cell above.*.
Tab ⇒ Finalize a cell entry and *move one cell to the right.*.
Shift + Tab ⇒ Finalize a cell entry and *move one cell to the left*.

Working With Data in Cells

ESC ⇒ Cancel a cell entry. Remove squiggy lines after a Copy.
Ctrl + Z or **Alt + Backspace** ⇒ Undo the last action. Can be pressed multiple times to undo multiple actions.
Ctrl + Y ⇒ Redo the last action.
Ctrl + K ⇒ Insert a hyperlink.
Double-click in a cell or **Click + F2** ⇒ Edit cell contents directly in the cell.
Ctrl + D ⇒ Fills down. Type a value in a cell and press Enter. Then click in the cell and, keeping the left mouse button pressed, move down the column x number of cells and release. Press **Ctrl + D**, and the value in the first cell copies to the other cells.
Ctrl + R ⇒ Fills right. Type a value in a cell and press Enter. Then click in the cell and, keeping the left mouse button pressed, move to the right x number of cells and release. Press **Ctrl + R**, and the value in the first cell copies to the other cells.
Ctrl + ` ⇒ Toggles between Excel displaying cell values and displaying cell formulas. This is helpful if you need to repeat a formula you typed elsewhere in the worksheet and can't remember it. The left apostrophe key is located to the left of the number 1 on many keyboards.
Ctrl + 1 ⇒ Excel opens the Format Cells window.
Ctrl + C ⇒ Copy the selection to the Clipboard.
Ctrl + V ⇒ Paste the selection from the Clipboard.
Ctrl + X ⇒ Cut the selection.
Ctrl + Spacebar ⇒ Select the entire column.
Shift + Spacebar ⇒ Select the entire row.
Ctrl + A ⇒ Select all cells in the spreadsheet.
Ctrl + B ⇒ Format the selection with Bold.
Ctrl + I ⇒ Format the selection with Italics.
Ctrl + U ⇒ Underscore (underline) the selection.
Ctrl + ; ⇒ Ctrl plus a semicolon inserts the current date from your computer.
Ctrl + Shift + : ⇒ Ctrl plus the colon key inserts the current time from your computer.

Ctrl + ; (press the spacebar) **Ctrl + Shift + :** ⇒ These two shortcuts together, separated by a space, insert the date and time in a cell.

Alt + 0162 (numeric keypad only) ⇒ Enter the ¢ (cent) symbol in a cell.

Alt + 0128 (numeric keypad only) ⇒ Enter the € (euro) symbol in a cell.

Alt + 0163 (numeric keypad only) ⇒ Enter the £ (pound sterling) symbol in a cell.

Alt + 0165 (numeric keypad only) ⇒ Enter the ¥ (yen) symbol in a cell.

Moving Around the Excel Worksheet

Home ⇒ Move to the beginning of the row.

Ctrl + Home ⇒ Move to the beginning of the worksheet.

Ctrl + End ⇒ Move to the bottom right corner of the worksheet.

Alt + Page Down ⇒ Move one screen to the right.

Alt + Page Up ⇒ Move one screen to the left.

Working With Excel Workbooks

Ctrl + F ⇒ Open the Find window.

Ctrl + H ⇒ Open the Replace window.

Ctrl + S ⇒ Save the workbook or Excel file. Get into the habit of pressing this key sequence often so you won't accidentally lose your work.

Ctrl + P ⇒ Open the Print window.

Ctrl + W or **Alt + F4** ⇒ Close the workbook or Excel file.

Ctrl + O ⇒ Open an existing workbook or Excel file.

Ctrl + N ⇒ Open a new workbook or Excel file.

Using Auto Fill Features

We will focus primarily on the **Fill Handle** - a powerful tool used right inside the worksheet! We also briefly show how these same functions can be accomplished via the ribbon in newer versions of Excel. In our example worksheets we fill columns top to bottom. But columns can be autofilled moving up a column, and rows can be autofilled. Tip: Always check the auto fill results. If a error is made, click the "Undo" icon at the top of the spreadsheet and try again. Excel provides two basic auto fill options: lineal series and growth series. These are very easy to understand even if you don't like math, so let's get started!

How to Auto Fill Using the Fill Handle

The easiest example of a linear series of numbers is 1,2,3,4,5. In a linear series, the next number in the series is always obtained by adding a constant, or **step value** to the previous number. Said another way, each subsequent number is incremented by the same value.

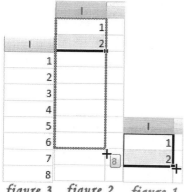

figure 3   figure 2   figure 1

A linear series can consist of decimals (1.5, 2.5, 3.5, 4.5), decreasing values (100, 98, 96, 94), or negative numbers (-1,-2,-3,-4). But in each case we ADD (or subtract) the constant or step value.
Let's see how we can autofill a column using the **Fill Handle**.

1. Open the Excel worksheet. In the first cell enter 1, and enter 2 in the cell immediately below.
2. Highlight the two cells, and hover the cursor over the **bottom right corner until you see the Fill Handle (+)** - see figure 1.
3. Press the LEFT mouse button and **drag down the column as far as you want Excel to auto fill** - see figure 2.
4. Release the mouse button and Excel fills the column with the linear series as shown in figure 3.

Alternate Option

If you want a linear series with a step value of 1, you can enter the first number only, click and drag the Fill Handle with the RIGHT mouse button, and click **Fill Series** on the small menu that displays. The default step value for **Fill Series** is one. If you have trouble using the Fill Handle, you may accomplish the same task using the **Fill button** on the Editing section of the ribbon's Home tab (Excel 2007 and higher). To use the Fill button on the ribbon:

1. Enter the two numbers in the worksheet.
2. Highlight these numbers and the rest of the column you want auto filled.
3. Click the **Fill Button**, and click Series.
4. In the Series window, make sure "Linear Series" is selected with a step value of 1, and click OK.

More Examples of Auto Fill of a Linear Series

Let's look at some other examples of using the Fill Handle to autofill numbers or other data in an Excel worksheet. Look at the sample worksheet below. In each case we entered the first two numbers or other data, and dragged the Fill Handle with the left mouse button.

- Odd numbers: When the first two numbers are entered, Excel knows that the step value is 2 and autofills the column with odd numbers.
- Every 4th number: In this example the step value is 4, so beginning with 2 and 6, Excel continues to increment each subsequent number by 4.
- Multiples of 5: The Fill Handle is handy for creating multiples of a number. Multiples are when each number can be *divided evenly* by the first number ... which is also the step value in our example.
- Thousands: Excel autofills by thousands as our step value is 1000.
- Months, time, and days: The last three columns illustrate Excel's capability of auto filling a variety of data series.

D	E	F	G	H	I	J	K	L	M
Data entered in 1st two rows			1	2	5	1000	Jan	8:00 AM	Monday
and then Fill Handle used.			3	6	10	2000	Feb	9:00 AM	Tuesday
			5	10	15	3000	Mar	10:00 AM	Wednesday
			7	14	20	4000	Apr	11:00 AM	Thursday
			9	18	25	5000	May	12:00 PM	Friday
			11	22	30	6000	Jun	1:00 PM	Saturday

Autofilling Linear Series and Skipping Rows

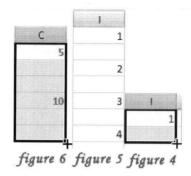

figure 6   figure 5   figure 4

It is not uncommon to skip rows in a busy worksheet to enhance readability. To have Excel autofill every "nth" row with a linear series with a step value of one, we have found that only one number usually needs to be entered, though Microsoft recommends always entering a minimum of two numbers. Be sure to always check the auto fill results for accuracy. Figures 4 and 5 show an example of autofilling numbers **every other row**. Enter the number 1, highlight that cell and the one below, then click the Fill Handle with the left mouse button, drag, and release. Excel autofills every other row (figure 5). Figures 6 shows how we highlight for the Fill Handle to have Excel autofill every third row. If we were autofilling 1,2,3,4, etc., only the first number would need to be entered. But in this example we are autofilling with multiples of 5, so we must enter the first two numbers in our series so Excel can determine the step value. Then we must remember to highlight the appropriate number of blank cells, five in this example, AFTER the second number.

Autofill a Growth Series (Geometric Pattern)

In the first section we learned that each number in a linear series is calculated by **adding** the step value to the previous number. In a growth series, the next number is obtained by **multiplying the previous number by the step value** (or constant). We will look at two methods for instructing Excel to autofill with a growth series or geometric pattern.

Method #1: Enter First Two Numbers in the Series

Specifying **growth series** in newer versions of Excel is easy. The fastest way is to enter the first two numbers and then **right-click on the Fill Handle**.

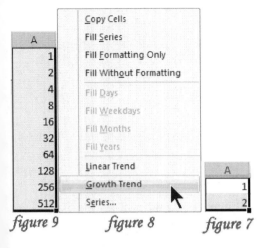

figure 9   figure 8   figure 7

In this example we have Excel autofill a worksheet column with a step value of 2.

1. In the Excel worksheet, enter 1 in the first cell and 2 in the cell immediately below. See figure 7.
2. Highlight the two cells, and hover the cursor over the Fill Handle (+).
3. Press the RIGHT mouse button, drag down the column, and release. The menu shown in figure 8 appears. Click **Growth Trend**.
4. Because you entered two numbers, Excel knows that the step value is 2. The autofill results are shown in figure 9.

If you want a step value of 3, enter 1 and 4 into the column. What if you want a step value of 2, but you want the series to begin with the number 3? You would enter 3 and 6 because 3x2=6. You must enter two numbers to use this quick method. If you only enter one number, the "Growth Trend" option is grayed out. Now let's look at Method #2.

Method #2: Enter the First Number and Specify the Step Value

The second method entails an extra step, but it is nifty. The four images below show our process of creating a growth series beginning with the number 1 and having a step value of 3.

1. Enter number 1 in the cell. Highlight the cell, click and hold on the Fill Handle with the RIGHT mouse button, and drag.
2. When the mouse button is released a menu appears. Click **Series** at the bottom of the menu.
3. The **Series window** opens. Type 3 in the **Step value** box and click **Growth** in the "Type" section. Click OK.
4. Excel fills the column as shown in the last image below.

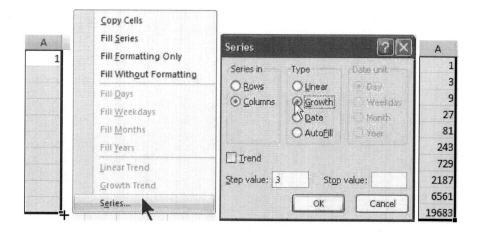

Using the Ribbon to Open the Series Window

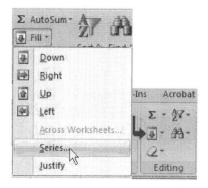

One can also reach the **Series window** shown above via the ribbon in newer versions of Excel. Note: The Fill Handle is NOT used in this method of reaching the Series window.

1. After the number 1 has been entered, click back in the cell and highlight it and the cells below it that you want autofilled.
2. With the column highlighted, click the **Fill button** located on the Editing section of the Home tab as shown in the image at right.
3. A dropdown menu appears as shown in the second image to the right. Click **Series** and the Series window appears.

Autofilling Dates (Days, Weekdays, Months, and Years)

We can instruct Excel to autofill cells with dates using the Fill Handle "right-click" function or via the Fill button on the ribbon. The Fill Handle is faster and we show an example. The Fill button has a bit of extra functionality which we explain below.

Autofill Dates with the Fill Handle

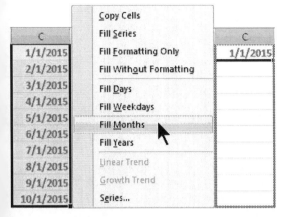

Below is an example of using the Fill Handle to autofill dates.

1. Type the beginning date in the cell. For our example, we've entered the first day of the year.**Right-click on the Fill Handle** and drag down the column.
2. When the mouse button is released, a menu displays as shown in the first image. We select Months in our example.
3. Excel autofills the column with the first day of each consecutive month as shown.

Autofill Dates with the Fill Button on the Ribbon

The Fill button can also be used to autofill dates with more functionality. It not only creates a series based on the unit you select, but it increments that unit (days, months, etc.) by the number entered in the "Step value" box. For example, after entering the first date and highlighting the column cells, click the **Fill button** and click **Series** from the dropdown menu that appears. When Dates is selected on the Series window (shown in the last section), the date unit is selected on the right side of the window. The step value default is 1, but you may select any value. For example, if you want every other month autofilled, enter a step value of 2.

Functions that we illustrated using the Fill Handle can also be accomplished using the Fill button on the ribbon. However, using the Fill button take more steps and is more time consuming, so we recommend using the Fill Handle when possible. Also, the Fill button on the ribbon has additional, albeit less common functions.

Creating A Chart

An Excel chart may be created and placed inside of a spreadsheet (worksheet) next to the data, or placed in its own spreadsheet. Excel charts can also be copied to other software programs such as PowerPoint.

Selecting Data for an Excel Chart

	A	B	C	D	E	F
1		1st Qtr	2nd Qtr	3rd Qtr	4th Qtr	Year
2	Flowers	$ 170	$ 240	$ 200	$ 230	$ 840
3	Shrubs	$ 220	$ 280	$ 250	$ 290	$ 1,040
4	Trees	$ 260	$ 340	$ 200	$ 320	$ 1,120

First, select the cells that contain the values you want shown in the chart. Click and drag the cursor from the top left cell to the bottom right cell of the worksheet - including column and row headings when possible. If your worksheet has a Totals column like in our worksheet above (e.g. Year), this data is typically not charted. Non-contiguous rows and columns of cells can be selected by pressing and holding the Ctrl key while selecting each group of cells. A data series is a related set of data points. In the image above, we selected a single series, Flowers. It is outlined in red. Many chart types allow us to plot multiple series. If we had selected Flowers, Shrubs, and Trees, we would be charting 3 series.

How to Create a Chart in Microsoft Excel

After selecting the cells, follow the steps below *for your version of Microsoft Excel* to create the chart.

Create a Chart in Excel 2007 and Newer Versions

Note: In the new versions of Excel, hover the cursor over a chart type or sub-type on the Insert ribbon to display a description of the chart.

- Click the Insert tab.
- Click the chart type from the Charts section of the ribbon. The sub-type menu displays.
- Click the desired chart sub-type. The chart appears on the worksheet.
- If you want to create a second chart, click somewhere in the worksheet to "deselect" the current chart first, or the new chart will replace the current chart.

Create a Chart in Excel 2003, 2000, and 98

Note: In older versions of Excel, click the chart type or sub-type in the Chart Wizard to display a description of the chart.

- Click Insert | Chart. The Chart Wizard appears.
- Step 1: Click the desired chart type in the left column, and click one of the chart sub-types in the right column. Click Next.
- Step 2: Excel assumes you wish to keep the series data in rows. You may click "Columns" to see how the chart changes. When finished, click Next.
- Step 3: Type a chart title. If you wish to add a title for the axes, do so. Then click Next.
- Step 4: Excel assumes you want the chart placed on the worksheet. If you would like the chart placed in a new sheet, click the radio button, type a sheet name, and click Finish.

Choosing the Chart Type

The type of data to be charted usually determines the chart type. If multiple chart types can be used for your data, choose the chart type that will help the user best visualize the patterns and relationships between the data values. The 4 most popular chart types in Excel are described below, along with the best use of each chart type.

Type		Description	When to Use
Pie Chart		Displays the percentages of a whole for each member in a series.	Excellent chart for comparing values in a single series as percentages of a whole.
Column Chart		Using vertical columns, displays values for one or more series over time or other category.	This chart type is especially effective in comparing values for multiple series. The 3-D Column chart displays multiple series over three axes (X, Y, and Z).
Bar Chart		Displays values for one or more series using horizontal columns.	Though useful for single or multiple series, this chart type is especially effective in comparing a large quantity of values in a single series.
Line Chart		Displays values as equally spaced points connected with a line.	This chart is especially useful in displaying trends over time or other ordered category for single or multiple series of data.

© Copyright - Keynote Support

Deleting, Moving, and Resizing Charts

To select an existing chart, click on its border, or click in an empty space inside the chart. When selecting a chart, be careful not to click on an element inside the chart or that element will be selected instead.

How to Delete a Chart

To delete a chart that has just been created, click the Excel Undo button. To delete an existing chart, select the chart and press the Delete key, or right-click and select Cut.

How to Move a Chart

To move a chart to a different place on the worksheet, select the chart and drag it to the desired location. To move a chart to a new or different spreadsheet in the same workbook, select the chart, right-click, and select Move Chart. Then choose the sheet or type in a new sheet name, and click OK.

How to Resize a Chart

To resize a chart, select the chart and drag any of the chart's corners.

Excel Chart Helpful Hints

For best results, keep the Excel chart simple and uncluttered. It is better to use multiple charts to express patterns and relationships between data than to use one chart that is too busy and over-complicated. A colorful chart is ideal for online presentations or for printing on a color printer. But shades of gray are best for monochrome printing of charts.

Chart Types

Defining Data Series

A data series is a related set of data points. It is usually one row of data in an Excel worksheet with the associated column headings; or one column of data with the associated row headings. All chart types can plot both single and multiple data series **except the Pie Chart** - as you will see shortly. In the worksheet below, we have outlined in red a single series of data.

	A	B	C	D	E	F
1		1st Qtr	2nd Qtr	3rd Qtr	4th Qtr	Year
2	Flowers	$ 170	$ 240	$ 200	$ 230	$ 840
3	Shrubs	$ 220	$ 280	$ 250	$ 290	$ 1,040
4	Trees	$ 260	$ 340	$ 200	$ 320	$ 1,120

Figure 1: single series of data

In the worksheet below, we have outlined in red 3 series of data, we can select non-adjacent rows in the spreadsheet to chart by pressing and holding the Ctrl key as we highlight the rows and/or columns.

	A	B	C	D	E	F
1		1st Qtr	2nd Qtr	3rd Qtr	4th Qtr	Year
2	Flowers	$ 170	$ 240	$ 200	$ 230	$ 840
3	Shrubs	$ 220	$ 280	$ 250	$ 290	$ 1,040
4	Trees	$ 260	$ 340	$ 200	$ 320	$ 1,120

Figure 2: multiple series of data

The Pie Chart

A Pie Chart can only display *one series of data*. Excel uses the series identifier as the chart title (e.g. Flowers) and displays the values for that series as proportional slices of a pie. If we had selected multiple series of data, Excel would ignore all but the first series.

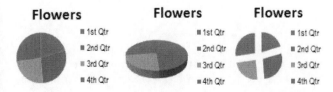

There are sub-types of the Pie Chart available. The second chart above is the Pie in 3-D and the third chart is an Exploded Pie Chart; an Exploded Pie in 3-D is also available. Several other sub-types include the Pie of Pie and Bar of Pie - in which a second pie is created from certain values in the first pie in order to emphasize them. To customize the values that the second pie contains, right-click on the segment in the first pie, select "Format Data Point," and specify how to split the series. Notice that the Pie Chart's legend contains the column headings from the worksheet. These can be changed by editing the headings in the worksheet, or by editing the chart directly. The legend can be moved to the top, bottom, left, right, or top right ("corner" in older versions of Excel) of the chart.

It is possible to customize the design of the pie chart so either the numeric values or the percentages display inside the chart on top of the slices of the pie.

The Column Chart

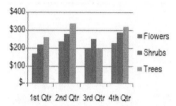

The Column Chart very effectively shows the comparison of one or more series of data points. But the Clustered Column Chart is especially useful in comparing multiple data series. In the chart at right, we plotted the data points in all three series: Flowers, Shrubs, and Trees. Because Excel uses a different color for each data series, we can easily see how a single series, Flowers for example, changes over time. But because the columns are "clustered," we can also compare the three data series for each time period.

In a Column Chart, the vertical axis (Y-axis) always displays numeric values, and the horizontal axis (X-axis) displays time or other category. The horizontal axis (X-axis) in our charts displays our time segments, and the series type (Flowers, Shrubs, and Trees) is plotted per time segment. Excel has designed the chart in this manner because the number of time segments (4) is greater than the number of series (3). Whichever has the highest quantity will be placed on the horizontal axis (X-axis).

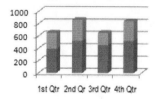

In other words, we could have Flowers, Shrubs, and Trees run along the X-axis, and the value of the four quarters plotted for each. One variation of this chart type is the Stacked Column Chart. We show a 3-D Stacked Column Chart at left. In a Stacked Column Chart, the data points for each time period are "stacked" instead of "clustered." This chart type lets us see the percentage of the total for each data point in the series.

Also available is the 100% Stacked Column Chart, where each value in a series is shown as a portion of 100%. An example of a 100% Stacked Chart is shown in the section on Bar Charts.

All the Column Charts have a version in which the columns display in three-dimension - as illustrated by the 3-D Stacked Column Chart above. But one chart, the "3-D Column Chart," is special because the chart itself is three-dimensional - displaying multiple series on the X-axis, Y-axis, and Z-axis. The first chart below is a 3-D Column Chart of our data series.

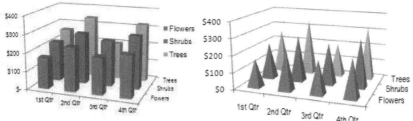

In newer versions of Excel, cylinders, pyramids, and cones can be used instead of bars for most of the Column charts. The second chart above shows a 3-D Pyramid Chart.

The Line Chart

The Line Chart is especially effective in displaying trends. In a Line Chart, the vertical axis (Y-axis) always displays numeric values and the horizontal axis (X-axis) displays time or other category.

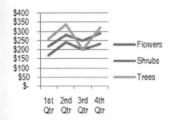

We selected the Line with Markers chart for our single series chart at left. You may choose each Line Chart type with or without markers. Markers are circles, squares, triangles, or other shapes which mark the data points. Excel displays a unique marker - different shape and/or color - for each data series. The Line Chart is equally effective in displaying trends for multiple series as shown in our chart at right. As you will notice, each line is a different color. This image shows a Line Chart without markers. Though not as colorful as the other charts, it is easy to see how effective the Line Chart in showing a trend for a single series, and comparing trends for multiple series of data values. Besides the Line Chart, we have the Stacked Line Chart and the 100% Stacked Line Chart - with or without markers. A 3-D Line Chart is available, but the Line Chart does not display data well in three dimensions.

The Bar Chart

The Bar Chart is like a Column Chart lying on its side. The horizontal axis of a Bar Chart contains the numeric values. The first chart below is the Bar Chart for our single series, Flowers.

When to use a Bar Chart versus a Column Chart depends on the type of data and user preference. Sometimes it is worth the time to create both charts and compare the results. However, Bar Charts do tend to display and compare a large number of series better than the other chart types.

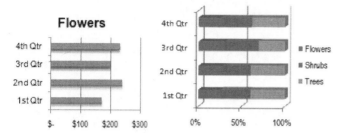

All of the Bar Charts are available in 2-D and 3-D formats, *but only the bars are 3-D.* There is no 3-D Bar chart containing three axes. As with the other chart types, Excel provides the Stacked Bar Chart and 100% Stacked Bar Chart. The second chart above is our 100% Stacked Bar Chart in 3-D. This chart type doesn't display currency on the horizontal axis, but percentages. It allows us to see what percentage each data point has out of 100%. As with the other chart types, new versions of Excel provide the option of using cylinders, pyramids, or cones instead of bars.

The Area Chart

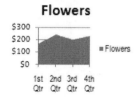

Area Charts are like Line Charts except that the area below the plot line is solid. And like Line Charts, Area Charts are used primarily to show trends over time or other category. The chart at left is an Area Chart for our single series.

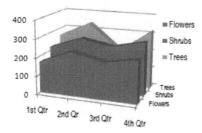

There are three charts available: the Area Chart, the Stacked Area Chart, and the 100% Stacked Area Chart. Each of these charts come in 2-D format and in true 3-D format with X, Y, and Z axes. The chart at right is our 3-D Area Chart, and effectively displays our three series.

In many cases, the 2-D version of the Area Chart can be ineffective in displaying multiple series of data meaningfully. Series with lesser values may be completely hidden behind series with greater values - as demonstrated in the first chart below. Flowers is totally hidden, and just a wee bit of Trees peaks through. Not a very effective chart! This problem does not occur in the Stacked Area Chart (shown below) or the 100% Stacked Area Chart.

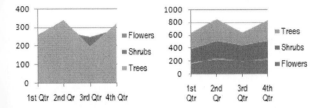

The Scatter Chart

The purpose of a Scatter Chart is to observe how the values of two series compares over time or other category. To illustrate the Scatter Chart, we will use the worksheet values shown below:

	A	B	C	D	E	F	G	H	I	J	K	L	M
1		Jan	Feb	Mar	Apr	May	Jun	Jul	Aug	Sep	Oct	Nov	Dec
2	Flowers	$100	$200	$300	$500	$600	$700	$550	$475	$700	$500	$350	$400
3	Shrubs	$200	$250	$400	$600	$700	$760	$650	$550	$775	$600	$275	$200

According to Scatter Plots (U. of Illinois), "Scatter plots are similar to line graphs in that they use horizontal and vertical axes to plot data points. However, they have a very specific purpose. Scatter plots show how much one variable is affected by another. The relationship between two variables is called their correlation."

The series pair has a Positive Correlation if they increase similarly, and a Negative Correlation if they both decrease in like manner. Otherwise, they have No Correlation. Excel does not use labels from the worksheet to label the horizontal axis; it just numbers the X-axis chronologically. The Scatter Chart comes in several different formats: markers can indicate the data points; and the points can be unconnected, or connected with smooth or straight lines.

Take a look at our two sample Scatter Charts below. The first chart is a Scatter Chart with Only Markers, and the second chart is a Scatter Chart with Smooth Lines. In general, markers work well when the number of data points is small, and smooth lines without markers are often used when the number of data points is large. But it is best to try the different sub-types to see which one best presents your data.

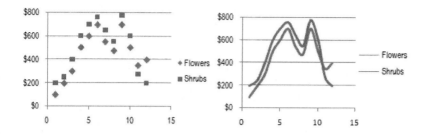

Other Chart Types

Excel offers other chart types, depending on your version, but the average user will not use these types of charts. Some of the other available chart types are: Stock, Surface, Doughnut, Bubble, and Radar.

Customizing Excel Charts

Creating a standard chart in Excel takes a minute, but customizing a chart can take a long time unless you follow a logical order. When Microsoft revised its Office products for the 2007 versions, it greatly enhanced the charting function. In some ways there are too many options.

Customizing Charts

Step 1: Getting Ready

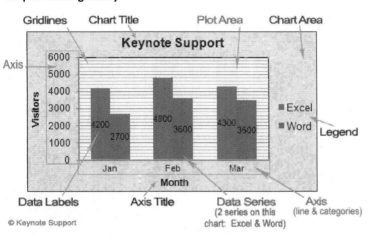

1. Become Familiar with Chart Terminology

Study the chart above to familiarize yourself with chart or graph terms. This will help you as you proceed through this tutorial.

2. Select a Color Theme

Every workbook has a "Color Theme" and chart colors are based upon the theme. All of Excel's pre-built styles are also based upon the Theme, so *change the Color Theme first!*
To view available Themes, click the Page Layout tab and on the "Themes" group, click Colors. Hover the cursor over each theme to view its colors on your chart. Click a theme to select it.

3. Select a Font Theme

Every Excel workbook has a default Font Theme also. If you want a different font for the majority of your chart text, change the theme now so all of the pre-built layouts and styles will display with your desired font.

Hint: DON'T change an element's font until the end of the customization process as clicking on a pre-built style changes the font back to the default. To set the Font Theme, click the Page Layout tab and on the "Themes" group, click Fonts. As your cursor hovers over a theme, your chart will display the theme fonts. Click on a Font Theme to select it.

Step 2: Determine the Overall Chart Layout and Style

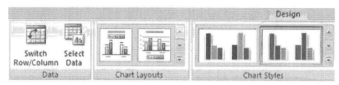

The first 3 customizing options for the chart layout are found on the Design ribbon.

1. Switch the Rows and Columns

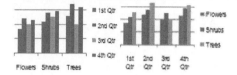

An Excel chart is drawn from selected rows and columns of data, and whichever has the most entries is charted on the X-axis (Y-axis for Bar Charts). In the first chart at right, the 4 quarters of the year display on the X-axis. We could tell Excel, however, to display the product types on the X-axis instead.
To make this switch, select the chart and click the Switch Row/Column icon on the Design ribbon. In the second chart, the product type now displays on the X-axis.

2. Select a Pre-Built Chart Layout

Excel provides pre-built Chart Layouts that contain different arrangements of your chart's elements. To view the layouts, select the chart and locate the "Chart Layout" section of the Design ribbon. On the right edge of the section are 3 arrows allowing you to view the layouts in different ways. Click on a layout to see its effect on your chart. Hint: To return to the original layout, **click the last layout on the dropdown menu**.

3. Select a Pre-built Chart Style
Using the colors in your workbook's Color Theme, Excel provides nearly 50 Chart Styles that recolor your chart differently. Some styles contain stylized borders or backgrounds.

To view available Styles, select the chart, click the Design tab, and find the "Chart Styles" group. On the right edge of the group are 3 vertically-aligned arrows. Click the bottom arrow to see the entire menu (see image). Then click on a style to see its effect on your chart. Hint: To return to the original style, **click the second style on the top row.**

Step 3: Adding Optional Chart Elements

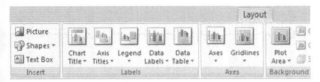

Five optional chart elements can be added via the "Layout" ribbon: a picture, prebuilt shape, text box, data table, and data labels. **To style these added elements, go to the next section.**

1. Insert a Picture, Shape, or Text Box on the Chart

Perhaps you would like to add comments, a logo, or a built-in shape to your chart. These options are available in the Insert group of the "Layout tab."

Picture: click the Picture icon. Select the picture from your hard drive and click Insert. Resize the image by moving its borders with the cursor. Images can be formatted manually via the right-click menu.
Text box and Shape: After clicking the Text Box or Shape icon, click in the chart and draw a box to hold the item. Enter your text in the text box. To customize, click on the item's border and select "Format Shape" from the right-click menu.

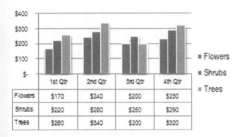

2. Display a Data Table

A Data Table contains the rows and columns of data upon which the chart is based. The chart at right contains a Data Table. Click the Data Table icon on the Layout ribbon and select the Data Table's placement from the options provided. Click "More Options" to customize.

3. Display Data Labels

Numeric values displayed on the chart series (e.g. columns) are called Data Labels. See the large chart at the beginning of this tutorial for an example. You can add Data Labels to all of the series in the chart in one step, or add Labels to individual Series. However, *styling* the labels must be done per individual series - which can be time-consuming!

To add Data Labels to all series, select the chart, click the Layout tab, click the Data Labels icon, and choose a position. Or click on a single series to add and position Data Labels for just that series.
To manually style a data series labels, click on one of the labels and select "Format Data Labels" from the right-click menu, or click the Data Labels tab on the ribbon and click "More Options."

Step 4: Formatting / Styling Individual Chart Elements

Listed below are hints and tips for customizing individual chart elements. Each element can be styled manually, *but each element also has a Shape Style*. So first let's learn what a "Shape Style" is, and then talk about the individual elements that can be customized.

Defining Shape Styles

New with version 2007, Excel provides a large selection of pre-built Shape Styles, based on the Color Theme, for each chart element. Found on the Format tab as shown above, Shape Styles contain variations of colors and effects for background, borders, and text.

How Do I Select a Shape Style?

First, select the chart element. To do so, either: 1) click on the element in the chart, or 2) click the Format tab, locate the "Current Selection" group, click the arrow on the top line, and choose an element. Regardless of the method, the selected element will display at the top of the "Current Selection" area. To select a Shape Style, click the bottom arrow next to the right-most "Abc" and view the entire menu of Shape Styles (see image at right). Hover the cursor over a style and watch the chart element change! Click on a Shape Style to select it.

1. The Data Series (Columns, Bars, or Lines)

Styling Data Series is time-consuming as *each series must be customized individually*; hence the importance of choosing a Color Theme and Color Style in the beginning.
To style a Data Series, click on a member of the series and select a Shape Style, or right-click for the format menu. To style one column, click on it twice.

2. The Chart Area

The Chart Area surrounds the Plot Area and extends to the edges of the chart. It can be filled with a solid color, gradient, image, or pre-built texture. Hint: Customize the chart's border via the Chart Area.
Select the Chart Area, preview the Shape Styles, and click the "Shape Effect" icon to style a border with cool features such as Glow and Soft Edges. Style manually via the right-click menu.

3. The Plot Area

The Plot Area, behind the gridlines, can have a customized background and border. Access the formatting menu via right-click, or by clicking the Plot Area icon on the Layout ribbon.

4. Gridlines

Click the Gridlines icon from the Axes section of the Layout tab. For each axis you can display no gridlines, Major Gridlines, Minor Gridlines, or both. Shape Styles are available, but the "More Options" menu provides additional styling options, such as caps and end arrows (depending on the chart type).

5. Axes

Clicking the Axes icon allows us to position or remove an axis; and possibly remove labels and tick marks, and customize number increments. Shape Styles are available, but the "More Options" menu provides additional styling options, such as text alignment and direction.

6. Text Labels

The first 3 buttons on the Labels section of the Layout ribbon provide for positioning and styling of the Chart Title, the Axes Titles, and the Legend. Before clicking "More Options," *preview the Shape Styles for these text labels*, and look at the other styling options on the Shapes Styles section of the ribbon.

Step 5: Fonts, WordArt, and Final Tweaking

Now we are ready for the finishing touches ... the final tweaking of our chart's layout and design.

1. Change Fonts

You selected the Font Theme in Step 1. But if you'd like to change fonts for a chart element, click on the element, right-click, and click Font.

For larger text, consider styling with WordArt - located on the Format tab next to the Shape Styles section. Select the text and select a "Quick Style;" or use the 3 vertically-aligned arrows on the right side of the WordArt group to fill, outline, and apply a special effect.

2. Moving and Resizing Chart Elements

Some elements can be moved, such as the Plot Area, Title, and Legend. Select the element, and when the cursor turns into a crosshairs, click and drag the element. To resize an element, hover the cursor over one of its sides until it turns into a two-sided arrow. Then click and drag the item's border.

Discount Excel Online Course

Why not take the Diploma in Excel course?

Click on the link below to get a mega discount as thanks for purchasing this book.

ttp://www.shawacademy.com/dynlanding/?code=RW5nIC1Qb3VuZA==&a_aid=562d2b416cc91&a_bid
773e93d0

Printed in Great Britain
by Amazon.co.uk, Ltd.,
Marston Gate.